Going to Orange

Diana Pearce

Going to Orange

In memory of my parents Ken and Phyl McGuffog

Going to Orange
ISBN 978 1 76109 503 0
Copyright © text Diana Pearce 2023
Cover image: Larisa Koshkina from Pixabay

First published 2023 by
GINNINDERRA PRESS
PO Box 3461 Port Adelaide 5015
www.ginninderrapress.com.au

Contents

Foreword	9
Unsettled Spaces	
Walk After Work	13
Spider	14
Pooh Sticks	15
New Year	16
Wharf Road Morning	17
Third Movement	18
The Beach	20
School Fire	21
Roadside	22
Renewal	23
Red Dust	24
Post-Dawn At Canterbury	26
Morning Transition	27
Helicopter	28
Frame	29
Corella Cafeteria	31
Threads	
The Gift	35
Summer Rain	36
Shearers Playing For a Bride	37
Requiem	38
Reflections	39
Pelicanus Conspicillatus	40
Overheard	41
Miseria	42
Kerosene Lamps	43
Ikebana	44

Flight of the Hang Glider	45
Dusk Flight	46
Flight Path	47
Drought	48
Division	49
Corrugated Iron	50
Collateral	51
Cleaning Day	52
Canary	53
Caesura	54
Winter Food	55
Tumult of Uncertainties	57
Still Life	59
Solitary	60
Sand	61
Salt	62
Leatherwood	63
Gully	64
Cinema Matinee	65

Shifts

Desiccation	69
Honour	70
High School Reunion	71
Spare Not	72
Moving the Ashes	73
Library Book	74
Collaged	75
Grandmother's Christmas Pudding	77
Beginnings	79
Tracks	81
The Sixth Age	82

Past Winters	83
Ghoolendaadi Woolshed	84
Farmyard Textiles	86
Winter Ride	87
Scarecrow	88
The Swing	89
The Piano	90
Necklaces	91
Rebuke	92
Homecoming	93
Circus	95
Acknowledgements	97
About the Author	98

Foreword

The poetry in this collection sees experience through the prism of ageing, and its themes are simultaneously biographical and universal. It moves from a country childhood to contemporary urban life.

The environment, loneliness, relationships, societal change – all are addressed through familiar activities, such as cleaning, an overheard conversation, a walk beside or through a park, school reunions or the loss of a friend. The poems' relative brevity belies their complexity.

This is a book reflective of times past and present, and of a country that is itself simultaneously both past and present. Diana Pearce is a poet who works strenuously, and successfully, to bring the life already lived into the life being lived now.

Ross Gillett

Unsettled Spaces

Walk After Work

The path had been restored,
an easy walk lined with trees,
their greenness blurred the concrete
of a nearby stormwater drain.

I saw free-playing
dogs and small children,
three football-booted boys
in striped jerseys
fast-clattering to a picket-fenced
practice field,
voices shrill with anticipation.

In the fork of an ancient fig
a young man played
his guitar and sang, while
on another branch,
a friend filmed
this strange recital.

Surprised   I paused
listened   my walk forgotten.
I should have asked why
and clapped their nonsense,

today there is no song
only an absence.

Spider

There is a spider on my balcony,
inching its way on unseen threads,

across…sway…moist silk
catching dewdrops of light,

a translucent prison
for small creatures.

Dew vanishes under the sun
the web is quietly hidden.

What is trapped it can consume,
what is broken it can rebuild.

Pooh Sticks

I stand on a concrete bridge
that crosses a tidal
stormwater drain,
I could play Pooh sticks here,

toss twigs into water
watch as they float
hope for a winner
tide in…tide out.

When I played
my last game
I didn't understand
life's ebb and flow.

New Year

Uncrowded shopping aisles,
telescoped waiting trolleys,
car parking easier.

He leans on the edge
of an oversized rubbish bin
sand-planted with butts,
smokes a tattered cigarette.

Wisps of white hair protrude from a knitted hat,
untrimmed beard, yellowed and greying,
clothes stretch, unwashed,
over a large ash-scattered belly.

A leftover from Christmas.

Wharf Road Morning

sunrise   blurred
along a sill of mist
at the harbour entrance

faint silhouette of a foredeck
a smudge of tugs
all seemingly immobile

a freighter   perhaps
carrying exotica
with promised pleasures

an ocean liner with
tourists   eager for a day
of exploration

a coal carrier
its holds filled
with darkness from the ground

in the rising sun's warmth
mist dissipates
the ocean is blank

Third Movement

Sydney Opera House, 11 March 2011

In a concert conversation,
brief mention of a news item
'severe earthquake off Japan'

words soon forgotten
when Mahler's symphony
envelops all.

Its third movement
a scherzo of mechanical
distorted rhythms with
hints of *a child's fear of the dark
unnerving dreams*
relieved in the final
two movements
by music of *tenderness*
and *broad daylight.*

After the concert
we watch water taxis
skip lightly on silver floes,
behind us the city,
a collage of light and dark.

We cannot hear
the other opus
far to our north

played by a wilful orchestra
to a musical score
of broken rhythms, false notes
unpredictable atonality.

Note: italics indicate quotations from the concert program notes.

The Beach

Above the riderless waves that break
like white robes across the rocks
a lone skua wheels on autumn's air.

Sheltered between the sandstone cliffs
a narrow stretch of buttery sands
damp-fringed by an ebbing tide.

Snugged against one cliff side
the local surf club,
doors shut, its guardians gone.

A gossip of gulls
scrabbling for scraps
on an empty beach

filled by two words
STAY HOME
gouged deep
into the sand,
impervious to a blustery wind.

School Fire

Vandals ride the hot west wind,
watch flames as they
listen to sirens singing.

Children's paintings
coloured by their world
dance, curl, die.

Bewildered children
are bussed to other schools,
lessons blurred through tears

while smoke-smudged words
limp with water,
float on a grey stream.

Roadside

A body rolls against
the freeway wall

my foot hesitates
about to brake

no, only a toy bear
in a white cardigan

a child's comfort
lost, rolling along

buffeted by passing cars,
unlike the new bears

sitting among the flowers
at death sites.

Renewal

I smell the dusts of demolition,
watch long shadows
creep across green spaces,
listen to children's voices
echoing in high-rise canyons.

At night I dream of houses
I no longer remember.

Red Dust

(a) Visible from space

Satellite images showed a red band sweeping across the east coast (NSW) and out to sea – *Sydney Morning Herald* 23/11/18

City sunrise,
orange-red light filters
through blinds that open
to a waterless fog;

dust
carried by winds
lifted from lizard-skin
river beds,
desiccated farmlands
and fading hope.

(b) Found Poem

From 'Done and Dusted not quite' – *Sydney Morning Herald* 23/11/18

Classed as hazardous,
extra paramedics rostered on.

Airport affected,
single runway operations only.

International and domestic
flights delayed   cancelled.

Gale force winds
are whipping up that dust,

lifting it aloft and just
steadily marching east.

Post-Dawn At Canterbury

The racecourse is quiet today,
ghost-mists hover above the grass
in a slow retreat from the sun,
a birdless pond glimmers silver.

No longer
the preening confidence
of an alertness of horses,
no passing shower of cheers
from weekday punters.

Indoors, vacant spaces fill
with the hum of empty escalators,
small television sets
play loops of past races
over and over and over.

To the south
a predation of single-armed
steel cranes
watch in silence.

Morning Transition

in the primitive time
the cold before
night's dreams subside

the cries start
from tree to tree
roof to roof

a gargle of magpies
the rasp of crows
pigeons' burred gossip
kookaburras' cacophony
all waiting for the answer
the truth   the right call

I open the curtains
mountains sharp against the horizon
sky of seagull grey and pink

a ship's lament
buses groan   motors roar
as lights turn to green

ink-grey clouds scatter
like bad news across
a clear sky

dawn's conversations cease
dreams forgotten

Helicopter

in midday stillness
a lone creature

churns vertically
into shimmering air

harsh percussion
an unease of sound

it hovers
under translucent halo

angles its bulk
swings   dips away

undertones
persist in
unsettled space

Frame

Click-clack rhythms
of a skateboard
on a graffitied curve
fill the post-dawn air.

The tide is out.

A young man stands
on a wooden bridge
across a concrete drain,
his back to the water-glistens
of the bay.

Grass struggles
under wispy casuarinas,
old tram sheds stand
empty.

He says, *What a place
to make a film!*

I pause, watch him,
director-like, he frames his hands,
So right!
Look at the sky!
Look at the space!
The light!

I turn
and see

stretches of still damp grass
an early pink-grey sky
the whitening moon.

Corella Cafeteria

Seen distantly they are
magnolia flowers,
blooming in the foliage
of large figs and plane trees,

they swoop above me;
a strident cloud.

As I cycle on a stationary bike
I view them at their breakfast
through the gym's window;

a flutter among twigs
that bend and rock
under their weight.

I watch their search
for small berry-like figs,
a smorgasbord hanging
there at summer's end.

I ignore my cycling target,
envy their precarious balance;
one talon grasping a child-sized
finger of swaying twig,
while their curved beaks feast.

I walk home,
crunching across a carpet
of twigs and leaves,
underneath the discord
of the well-fed.

Threads

The Gift

A cello, newly made,
brought across oceans
for a governor's lady.

Like a child
safe in its mother's embrace,
it cleaves to her
as she leans into its neck,
draws a new bow across
virgin strings
and fills a celibate body
with song,
mothers' laments for children lost
in histories of raids
and ancient rivalries,
newly learnt court music
played in small salons.

Muted tones
drift across harbour waters,
caress a vast and awe-full land
with alien sounds
that, perhaps, soothe
a man who sees
beyond ochrous sandstone,
khaki trees and penal codes,
a different bequest.

Summer Rain

After Angus Nivison, Newcastle Art Gallery, 2019

I sit on our veranda
listen to rain's timpani on the iron roof
its chorus in the tanks' overflow

breathe the dampness in the air
watch water cascade
like shafted light

see it become blood
as it scours the tree-dead hillsides
of a distressed land

Shearers Playing For a Bride

After Arthur Boyd's painting

I wonder if she exists,
this virgin bride,
a bouquet of wildflowers
wilting in her hand.

She hovers at lamp's edge
a ghost at the shearing
quarters of men
too long from home

who disregard
their hard-earned wages
to gamble
on a white-draped dream,

that lives in the cards
they hold, hidden
like the thistle spines
buried below their skin.

Requiem

Sandy Hook Elementary School, 2012

Wintry silences.
On school shelves
picture books waiting,
display boards of
paintings bright
with children's worlds
hanging unseen.

Reflections

We row to where
tea trees edge the river banks
where their tannin stains the water
inky black.

In the mirrored quiet
of this windless morning
an underwater realm appears,
no beginning, no end.

Logs float on logs,
trees arch across water
meet dark sky underneath,
we look down
at shadowed familiar faces
in the world below.

The wind whispers
to the trees,
dark waters ripple
we are no more.

Pelicanus Conspicillatus

Flaps down,
the largest pelican
in the world

lands, feather-like
on a grey wooden bollard
at pier's end.

Black and white feathers fold,
beige-pink beak tucks
against curved body,
question-mark sculpture
framed against cobalt
sky and water.

If I move, will you
sweep across the water,
take flight,

ride thermals
carry that improbable
body on pterodactyl wings

while I remain
in my flightless life?

Overheard

'There are no fabric shops in Forbes, you have to go to Orange.'

In country towns the trucks stop,
refuel, refresh, restart,
unpicking the highway.

Past brown, quilted paddocks
and faded squares of yellow grass,
all bleached in harshest sun.

Woven through the land
are threads of life,
fabrics of an old society.

Miseria

after *The Widow 1*, Kathie Kollwitz, 1921

She is Queen Victoria
        Jacquie Kennedy
                Coretta Scott King
                      Naomi.

She stands at Christchurch
        Dunblane
                Sandy Hook
                      Port Arthur.

She is our mother
        daughter
                sister
                      friend.

Ahead
        a life-scape of darkness,
                no flesh to touch
                      no voice to hear.

Kerosene Lamps

They were the eyes of night,
glowing among dark silhouettes
of trees and houses
set back from country roads.

Families worked, ate and read
in diffused light
from lamps
whose flames were lit
on kerosene-soaked wicks,
their blaze enclosed in
Titian-curved glass chimneys.

I see one today,
its sinuous beauty,
its virgin wick coiled
in an empty glass bowl,
electric lights reflected
in every surface.

Ikebana

It's not where you put the flowers, he said,
it's the spaces in between
that matter.

Like pauses between
a symphony's movements,
your indrawn breath
and silent embrace of harmony.

Like elusive words
suspended
between thought and writing
while blank pages linger.

Like the hiatus
after a question asked,
face composed in
wordless response.

In this interval
before my life's final act,
I select memories,
arrange with care

leave spaces in between
for all else that has elapsed.

Flight of the Hang Glider

Great bird
leaps into emptiness,

I hear the gasp
of parting air.

Held by silken wings
his pod-like body

rides silent thermals
above a coruscation of waves

and long-bodied freighters
along the horizon.

I envy his freedom
as he glides and dips

among the updrafts,
until the cliff

takes him back to the earth
where sirens sing.

Dusk Flight

From my balcony
I watch flying foxes
dip past,
noiseless
close,
no birds
these black velvet
curves of flight
above the city's evensong.

Elsewhere
they hang,
fold into their wings,
speak in hacksaws of sound.

After this summer's cauldron
will they be glimpsed only in dreams
or felt in a frisson of air at dusk?

Flight Path

The planes prowl
circling, horizontal,
time-static sky walkers
above a city
still dark-shaped in dreams
of unknown people sleeping,

until the vivid light
of Helios rising
and curfew's ending.

Planes point downwards,
wheels lowered,
scream resistance in descent,
touch ground.

The god rises,
people wake.

Drought

Drought tiptoes on hot dry feet,
ears attuned to the tap-tap-tap
of knuckles on emptying tanks.

Drought smiles at the raucous jokes
of an old black crow,
pecking at the body of a dying sheep.

Drought drinks thirstily,
leaving dams and rivers dry,
her craving unquenched.

A harsh and selfish lover,
she succours her own infertility,
delighting in her barren womb.

Division

I unpack my dishwasher,
open the cutlery drawer

that contains a segregated society,
particular about the company it keeps.

I drop the knives unsorted,
leave them to their icy rigidity.

Dessert spoons topple defiantly…
fledglings, eager to leave their nestings.

Teaspoons, like two-year-old children,
tumble in careless abandon.

Servers, skewers, chopsticks and peeler
are misfits jumbled in one long alley way.

It's the forks I like,
taking comfort from their intimacy

curve to curve, tines dormant,
cold-fleshed lovers.

Corrugated Iron

It was part of our farm, our home,
its dune-like perfection
covered and protected everything.

Whole constructions of curved precision
became part of our landscape;
water tanks, barns, woolsheds,
Murcutt's prize winning architecture.

It was 'the white man's bark',*
the percussion of hail
tap-dancing on rooves,
rain's overtures.

Until the rains stopped,
the land dried and cracked,
lightning raked down
from waterless clouds,
the no-longer mythic dragons awoke.

Today, warped in its grief,
it covers what it could not protect.

* *World Archaeology*, Issue 28

Collateral

A response to George Gittoes exhibition, Newcastle Art Gallery, March 2020

Old wars and modern deprivations.

The dispossessed
sheltered only
between fragments
of lives once known,

some
palms skyward
in supplication,
others grief-rigid.

Eyes are voids,
hollowed
by the triumph
of destruction.

I leave,
step into sunshine.

Cleaning Day

the cedar table oiled
oak shelves and table waxed
pottery dusted
bathroom sanitised

a bouquet of lavender
beeswax and eucalypt
mingles with
an aroma of satisfaction

in the evening
a single light reflected
on polished wood
lights the empty chairs

the table laid for one

Canary

Miners carry songbirds
into the darkness,

as the sunshine fades
death is a wisp of gas.

Who makes music
in dark places?

Who sings
the last notes?

Caesura

I listen to
Gregorian chants,
I imagine candlelit faces,
and flickering shadows
across stone pillars
reaching to vaulted ceilings.

Fluttering
and agitated chirps
disrupt my peace,
an anxiety of mynahs
gathers on the roof opposite,

louder still,
discordant canticles
resound above trees
as, borealis-like,
corellas
dance, dip and turn,
harmony of movement
contradicting
inharmonious song.

As sudden as their visit
corellas vanish into silence,
chattering mynahs depart.
I am left with plainsong.

Winter Food

Only a .22 bullet needed
one shot, between the eyes
where the hair forms a star.

In the year we raised a bullock
our pet kangaroo adopted him,

no longer followed us
nor bothered our ponies,

instead, the two grazed,
inseparable, all spring and summer.

Each autumn on the cusp
of frosts and iciness

a bullock was killed,
meat shared among families.

When our bullock was led
to a small slaughter yard,

the kangaroo followed,
a safe distance from excited dogs,

he curved his body into the grass,
settled to wait.

By nightfall all was quiet,
a body hung hessian-covered,

a large hide dried
on wooden rails.

At sunrise
the kangaroo began his search,

visited all their shared places.
Each day he ignored us,

all our offers of food,
of gentle petting.

Our father found him
cold, under an old pine-tree

when winter's first frost
iced the ground.

Tumult of Uncertainties

Written after two severe attacks of vertigo

a primal roar   a taste of bile

the room waltzed
to an unheard Strauss
dip   two   three
whirl   two   three

fairground lights
flashed
        swirled

a tinkling carousel
up and around   down

                            down

around
        down
                down

the big dipper descended
open clowns' mouths gyrated

somewhere Stravinsky dissonance
played by a wayward orchestra

a river meandered
the ground fractured

I hurtled with the water
in a single plunge

unreachable depths
a disquieting past

I surged with the water
to a second drop
fell through a bouquet
                of dancing lights

down steep-sided gorges
rebounded
                fell again
I drifted on dark acidic waters
                      floated into a cul-de-sac

time shifted   on the wind
a car on oily roads
                where tides flow into
a void

my eyes opened
a tantrum of fireworks

I remained not sleeping
not waking
suspended between realms

waiting for a tranquil skyline

I emerged
                a swirling mist

Still Life

Life together
was a landscape
painted with small strokes

shared jokes, unfinished sentences,
warming bodies in cold beds,
a hushed rainforest walk.

The landscape's wooden frame
was gilded by delicate flakes,
brushed on by each day's passing.

Today the painting hangs,
cracked and dark,
frame tarnished.

A glimpse
of what we once knew.

Solitary

Your neighbour said,
Aren't you lonely?
You should try this website.

In the early
light of morning,
you wonder

no more
perfunctory exchanges
with strangers

no more
unshared afterthoughts
about movies, concerts

no more
cold breath of loneliness
on winter nights

You turn the radio on,
the forecast says *rain clearing*
a sunny day ahead.

Sand

In the cold time
neither sleeping nor waking
I hold the sands of our words
mould them   shape them
but they slip through my fingers
shift on the wind
to other dunes.

In the darkness
I will write them
on your eyelids
and you will read them
as you sleep.

Salt

We bought a house beside the sea,
toasted moonlight's corrugated path
across the waters.

When storms swept in
salt mist clung to glass,
seeped into the brickwork,

corroded the foundations,
old nails and hidden pipes
that kept us whole,

hung invisible in rooms,
like word-filled silences
between us.

When slivered moons shed
no light on dark waters
we sold the house,

but the salt remained
in our bones.

Leatherwood

Euchryphia lucida

He gave me a tin of honey
Special order, he said.

I lifted the lid,
distinctive unsweet perfume

of liquid blossoms
filled my senses.

I tasted the intensity
of white-petal nectar.

This year
the warmth of late spring

brought bitter
rain and winds.

Leathery sheaths unfolded,
their flowers fell

bees no longer fed.
I close the lid,
the tin is empty now.

Gully

Once there was no gully
just an unbroken landscape
of hope-filled words.

The trees were cleared
lands ploughed
crops and vegetables grew.

In the sometime flow of water
across dry and work-filled days
a gully fractured the land,

words and soil were lost
the banks became slippery
spaces too dangerous to cross.

Cinema Matinee

I sit in the back row
watch previews
interminable advertisements
sip coffee and wait.

Once…
a lush red curtain was drawn back
revealing pictures in black and white,

heroes dressed in white,
riding white horses,
singing as they
watched restless cattle
under endless prairie skies,

villains dressed in black,
riding in black-horsed gangs
smoking thin cigars
peering through narrowed eyes
sneering and patting side arms.

Victories were simple,
evildoers shot
good triumphant.

Today grey figures
walk city streets,
trench-coated,
watching through dark glasses,
ambiguities of roles
purposes unknown.

My coffee cup is empty.

Shifts

Desiccation

My country school reunion
was held at the end
of a drought-claimed summer,
its handiwork showing
when I drove past

desperations of gums,
gaunt limbs of
the already-dead held
in supplication
to a selfish water god.
Refreshed by a recent storm,
brown paddocks blushed
with a deceptive green.

We gathered,
a greyness of septuagenarians,
sharing faintly verdant
recollections of school life
decades past,
each a disparate memory
built into an imperfect whole.

At weekend's completion,
in the embrace of separation,
an aridity came
and stood between us.

Honour

gold lettering fades
on brown boards

High School Reunion

I went to my school reunion
saw old men walking
in the same direction,
I wondered who they were.

I too, paused at that well
of teenage years,
long-hidden
by life's undergrowth,

puzzled at a grotesquerie of faces
woven with threads of time
a distortion of wrinkles
as age claimed creped skin
on once-young bodies.

We recognised each other
in eyes and voices,
consummated a half-century
of waiting.

Silent last embraces,
no further dates planned.

Spare Not

A battle-scarred, century-old
wooden bread board
sits in my kitchen,
on it these two words
describe my grandmother's life.

> Small clothes, well-worn
> sewn to threadbare blankets,
> winter-warm rugs.
>
> Pale calico flour-bags
> boiled in coppers, softened
> to line rough woollen clothes.
>
> Scraps of soap, compressed
> in small empty cans,
> rainbow cleaners for working hands.

I still use
this small round board,
with its carved, fading
two-word reminder.

Moving the Ashes

We will move our parents' ashes.
We have all gone
to other places,
no visitors come,
no flowers in remembrance.

We will take their nameplates
to the town
where they met and married,
place them
with their ancestors
on the cemetery wall,

scatter their ashes at the farm
where our house now ghosts itself
on a gentle slope,
century-old pines
surround its silence.

Here their shades
will see rounded hills,
smell the smoke of
open fires and fuel stoves,
hear the fuss of roosting fowls,
a distant bark, a lamb's bleat,
feel the touch
of evening breezes.

Library Book

Anne of Green Gables by L.M. Montgomery

My one-room bush school closed
when I was ten.
I asked to keep a library book
bound in faded blue cardboard.

Between its pages I'd met a girl
who lived on an island I didn't know,
quoted poets I hadn't read,
transformed her landscapes
from ordinary to extraordinary.

Muddy dams, drab-green gums,
rocky outcrops and reed-filled creeks
filled my landscapes.
I read Banjo Paterson, Henry Lawson,
Dorothea Mackellar.

I wanted to transform my world
with lakes of shining waters,
Dryads' bubbles, haunted woods,
to read Tennyson, Keats and Coleridge,
to know of love lost and heroes found.

Today as I deliberate over
droughts or construction sites,
I still recall my inability
to make exotic the mundane,
my envy of Anne Shirley.

Collaged

I visited my friend
in rehabilitation,
brought my poems;
one of Bronte Beach
where our children played,
another of her walks
in the Botanical Gardens;
a contrast to newspaper headlines.

Her doctor had talked
of medications,
high and low function words,
numbers.
She smiled in retelling,
'Maths was never my forte.'

We'd knitted rugs for charity;
I asked, 'Can you still knit?'
She nodded, 'I brought wool with me.
My left hand is weaker but
I can still hold the needles.'

We sat in her beige ward,
ravelled our lives' strands;
how our daughters grew up together,
her home near the Gardens,
my poems, her politics,
solving cryptic crosswords,
food and education,
until they became
a multicoloured whole,
stitched together over decades.

On the day of her funeral
unseasonal rain flooded the streets,
stranding buses, cars, pedestrians.

Marooned at home, I sat alone
behind the floodmark,
wrapped in threads
of loss and loving.

Grandmother's Christmas Pudding

When September ends
I watch my grandmother
seated in the backyard
of my mind
making Christmas puddings.

She sits on a plain
stiff-backed wooden chair,
cradles a blue and white bowl
in her aproned lap.
She plunges one work-worn hand
deep into brown sugar
and home-made butter,
squeezes, batters and beats them
into a caramel-coloured
creaminess.

Blending complete,
she uses a large wooden spoon
as she adds eggs,
their yolks
becoming a silky translucence
over the velvet-sweet fusion.

The kitchen air is filled
with aromas of grated nutmeg,
ground cloves and cinnamon,
plump rum-soaked raisins,
small black currants and
drunken sultanas.
She folds all in with flour
then sows the fruited furrows
with small silver coins.

When all is combined
she ladles spoonfuls
onto square calico cloths
stained with maps
of every Christmas past,
ties each tightly into imperfect balls,
boils them in great black pots
on a large wood-burning stove.

Cooked at last, they hang
in the cement-cooled laundry,
dangling from S-hooks,
shrunken grey heads
waiting for Christmas.

Beginnings

Smoke-smudged skies,
January ends, school starts,
for father and child
a two-mile walk.

Landmarks noted,
a silent woolshed,
machines dormant
air redolent with stale odours
of lanolined wool and tar

single-file sheep tracks past
white quartz boulders
silicon gleaming in morning sun,
untracked ridges,
a large spreading gum tree

a bush road that passes
a pine-sheltered farmhouse,
dried stubble paddocks
filled with stooks of hay
ready for winter storing.

They look at their reflections
in a reed-filled pond holding
clouds of frogs' eggs,
he leaves her brief warnings:
beware of the Jersey bull
spur-winged plovers
and red-bellied black snakes.

There are no cautionary signposts
for the journey she starts
in a one-room school.

Tracks

Below pale summer skies
small towns and sidings
wait for trains whose parts rust
under cinnamon grasses,
wait for timber, baled wool
and eager travellers,
wait until dreams evaporate
under the sun's incandescence.

In midsummer eyes squint
along shimmering
distorted tracks,
lost fumes of burnt coal and diesel
intermingle with odours
of parched earth, tired grass
and traces of eucalyptus.

In the silence we listen
for the lonely cry of a forgotten train,
once heard as a child
when I peered into the darkness,
filled with a fearful excitement,
waiting for the braking scream
of a steam-wreathed Cyclops.

Now only the jarring shrill of cicadas
and rasping crows
bring life.

The Sixth Age

Title from Shakespeare, *As You Like It*, Act II, sc. vii

Clouds linger on the horizon
the autumn sun still shines.

These are the times for old people
to move through corridors of memories

before the skin is parched,
blood rusted, bones corroded.

Time to listen to the lyrics
below the clamour of days

time to find the wonder
in the still-to-come.

Past Winters

winter is the waiting time
time for conversations with my past
recollections like fantasies
in the embers of open fires

pale suns in faded denim skies
long nights, black frosts under starlight,
bitter mornings,
water pipes covered in hessian

dams edged with icy hoofprint puddles
knots of sheep and cattle sheltered
under pine tree windbreaks
sometimes in the south
a gathering of low, dark clouds

we wrapped ourselves in hand-knitted
woollen scarves, built a meagre snowman
in a grass-flecked coat
from morning's brush of snow

winter is the waiting time,
remembrances shift and tumble
like embers in an open fire

Ghoolendaadi Woolshed

This poem was inspired by two photos of the woolshed on Ghoolendaadi, Boggabri, NSW, one at the end of the nineteenth century, the other late twentieth century

Today the shed's door sags
shutters are empty-eyed
tall thistles line a broken fence
an old tank lists.

Large woolsheds
were new cathedrals
built across an old land.

My grandfather
was its gun shearer,
photographed there
with other unsmiling
shearers and shed hands
standing, arms folded
in front of that shed
with its curved roof
pristine walls,
shining water tank.

He toiled beside those men,
bending their backs over sheep,
clipping to remove fleeces
with hand-held shears

ignoring grass seeds buried
in lanolin-softened hands

listening to the chorus of kelpies
herding sheep into catching pens.

In the lull of morning breaks
they ate scones, drank strong billy tea
rolled smokes,
swapped stories of other sheds.

In the stillness of the disused shed
we breathe the incense of their labour.

Farmyard Textiles

On the farm
fetid animal pelts
air-dried;

short-fleeced sheepskins
                arrayed and parched
                on wooden rails,

rabbit skins, fur inwards
                stretched taut over
                parabolic wires,

kangaroo skins
                in browned crucifixion
                on a wooden granary wall.

Sun-dried drapes
                collected, then traded –
                children's pocket money.

Winter Ride

Frost, deep and sharp,
defies the morning sun
chills the children's fingers
as they bridle
their winter-coated ponies
and wrestle icy buckles
on cold leather saddles.

They ride their ponies
through crystal grasses
past opaque, iced puddles
to a small schoolhouse
in a silvery paddock.

In the winter of my life
my hands slowly
return to the clasp
that once held the reins.

Scarecrow

Inflexible I stand
a scarecrow
clad in yesterday's words.

Will scattered seeds
sown in my mind
take root
before crows of doubt
ransack the furrows?

I am a scarecrow
regarding barren fields.

The Swing

It hangs from an elm branch
  thick ropes
    wooden seat worn shiny,
      I sit, a minor shift
        in protest,
          as I tug hard
against inertia,
              reach out to the hanging
                leaves, green and tempting
              stretch   stretch
              each swing higher
                each swing futile.

                        Leaves
                    are my poems
                    suspended just
                      beyond my
                      extended
                        words.

The Piano

For Eloise and Felicity

The great-granddaughters said it had to stay

the century-old simple upright
ivory keys yellowed
holes where once brass candle-holders sat
tuning still viable.

Once played by their great-grandfather
until his fingers, thickened by
shearing, wood cutting, potato bagging
lost their touch.

Their great-grandmother kept playing;
a respite at day's end
harmonies blending with scuffles
of birds roosting, a sleepy dog's bark.

Today, inside the aged timbers,
the silent reverberation
of strings holding melodies;
hymns and wartime songs,
ragtime and the tentative notes
of young fingers
light on the keys.

Necklaces

I'd gathered up the tumbles
from broken necklaces;
coloured shells, polished rocks,
small imitation pearls and broken clasps,
carefully bagged the parts.

The necklace maker said
I'll do my best.

I wear them again,
reordered, replaced,
like memories,
some the same
others are fragments
strung to make a different whole.

Rebuke

Beside a sandy track
a large lizard suns itself.

The children grab
sticks, fist-fitting stones.

At their first blows
the creature turns, stunned

faces its tormentors,
blue tongue emerges.

Shrieks of delighted fear
shrill higher in attack.

For days,
faces averted,

they hurry past
its ant-ridden corpse.

Homecoming

I go back,

see unchanged soft hills
in a mist of clouds,
undertones of winter
in browned autumn grass.

Stop opposite
an empty paddock,
its small entrance gate,
chained shut,

before me,
grey with age,
a solitary shed,
a fragment of a fowl yard.

I close my eyes
yesterday no longer distant;

a veranda-shaded farmhouse
nestles behind pine-trees,
wraiths of smoke from its chimney,

my mother roasts mutton
and home-grown vegetables
on a black fuel stove,

my father counts sheep
hurling themselves to freedom
from catching yards,

my brother and I unsaddle ponies
after riding home
from a one-room school.

I leave,
shadows linger
in an autumn sun.

Circus

Once a year it arrived
in our town, in trucks
heralding its name,
caravans covered
in mystic signs and bold colours,
prime movers towing animal cages.

In the daytime we saw
elephants, chain-tethered,
caged lions and tigers
caught between an insanity
of small prowling
and yawning indifference,
serious-faced monkeys tied
outside the vans
and a fortune teller's tent.

At night all became magic
as we sat on tiered
long wooden seats,
ate the sugary melt of pink fairy floss,
smelled the newly spread sawdust,
the not-quite-fresh canvas
of the single-ringed tent.

We clapped bareback riders standing
in glittering sequinned tights
on ornately bridled white horses,

gaped at the breath-altering trapeze artists,
all glitz and dusting powder
swinging above
a brown-roped safety net,
seemingly inadequate
for a death-stop.

After the lions roared
at their whip-cracking trainer
we then laughed, anxiety relieved,
at dogs walking on hind legs,
the absurdity of clowns
with oversized red mouths
tossing confetti
out of water buckets.

When we fell off our own horses
as we tried to stand on them,
landed awkwardly when we twisted
off our swing,
failed to make our kelpies
walk upright,
we knew
the circus was indeed
the greatest show on earth.

Acknowledgements

Published

'Pelicanus Conspicillatus' and 'Desiccation', *Blue Giraffe 13* mid-year 2014, *Blue Giraffe 14* mid-year 2015, guest editor Peter Hay, Blue Giraffe Press

'Canary', People of the Valley, *Writings from the Hunter*, Catchfire Press 2009, Commended

'Sand,' 'Small Suburban Crimes', *UTS Writers Anthology* 2001

'Dusk Flight' and 'Corrugated Iron', *Messages from the Embers* anthology, editors Julia Kaylock and Denise O'Hagan, Black Quill Press 2020

'The Library Book', *Writers Voice*, FAW NSW Inc. Spring edition 2020

Awards

'Drought', Second Prize, Yarram Community Learning Centre 2009

'Overheard', Highly Commended, Eyre Writers Award 2010

'Tracks', Highly Commended, FAW (Vic.) Mornington Peninsula Prize 2011

'The Gift', Commended, Eyre Writers Awards 2013

'Requiem', Commended, FAW (Vic.) Mornington Peninsula Prize 2013

'Third Movement', Third Place, Ethel Webb Blundell Literary Awards 2014

'Moving the Ashes', Second Place, FAW (Eastwood/Hills) 2014

The Mozzie

Many of the poems in this collection have been published in the *The Mozzie*, whose editor, Ron Heard, says of Diana, 'You have your own voice, an original way of seeing and a feeling for words.'

About the Author

Diana Pearce is a retired primary school principal. Following her retirement, she completed a Masters degree at UTS. Her final subject included a collection of her poems.

The everyday inspires her work: urban development, childhood memories, domestic activities and her environment.

She was awarded a mentorship from the Hunter Writers' Centre with Ross Gillett. She continues to work with him as well as participating in local workshops and online courses run by the Writers Centre at Rozelle (Sydney).

www.ingramcontent.com/pod-product-compliance
Lightning Source LLC
Chambersburg PA
CBHW050306120526
44590CB00016B/2509